ALL
AROUND TOWN

The Photographs of Richard Samuel Roberts

This book is for
Richie Ross, Taelor Marie Johnson, Trey Irby, Chymere Hayes,
and Niani Sekai Feelings,
whose mighty spirits
give me joy and hope

Henry Holt and Company, LLC, *Publishers since 1866*
175 Fifth Avenue, New York, New York 10010 [mackids.com]

Henry Holt® is a registered trademark of Henry Holt and Company, LLC

Library of Congress Cataloging-in-Publication Data
Johnson, Dinah. All around town : the photographs of Richard Samuel Roberts / by Dinah Johnson.
Summary: Chronicles the rich lives of the African American citizens of Columbia, South
Carolina, as well as other towns and cities during the 1920s and 1930s.
1. Photography—South Carolina—History—Juvenile literature. 2. African Americans—
South Carolina—Pictorial works —Juvenile literature. 3. Roberts, Richard Samuel, d.
1936—Juvenile literature. 4. African American photographers—South Carolina—
Juvenile literature. [1. Photography—History. 2. African Americans—Pictorial works.
3. Photographers. 4. Roberts, Richard Samuel, d. 1936. 5. African Americans—
Biography.] I. Roberts, Richard Samuel, d. 1936. II. Title.
TR24.S6 J65 1998 779.092—dc21 97-16682

ISBN 978-0-8050-5456-9 / First Edition—1998
Designed by Meredith Baldwin

Printed in China by South China Printing Company Ltd., Dongguan City, Guangdong Province
10 9 8 7 6 5 4

ALL AROUND TOWN

The Photographs of Richard Samuel Roberts

Dinah Johnson

Henry Holt and Company   New York

Mr. Richard Samuel Roberts
took pictures all around town—

Of college graduations

And for birthday party invitations

Of weddings

And of baseball teams

Of people working hard

Of schoolgirls exercising on the lawn

Of gingerbread houses

And fancy cars.

Mr. Richard Roberts
made perfect pictures.

That's what the sign said at
1119 Washington Street,
in Columbia, the capital of
South Carolina.

That's where people posed, most times in their Sunday-go-to-meetin' clothes.

Here's a beautiful little baby with a bow;

Two handsome brothers
with their scooters.

Six musicians with their instruments.
Would you like to hear their favorite song?

Do you see the
black-eyed dog
with this man?

Is this a pet chicken?

The grandson of
one of these women
just might have grown
up to be an astronaut.

And this one playing
cowboy might have
become a judge when
he was a big man.

With her apron on this lady was a maid.
But without it she was a mother,
the best singer in the choir, a neighbor.
A woman with dreams.

This woman might have been a strict but loving teacher.

Here's a kind and caring preacher.

This man was a maker of movies.

Wasn't she sassy!   Wasn't he sharp!

Here's a picture of
a proud papa.

Mr. Richard Roberts and his wife,
Wilhelmina, were proud parents, too.

Mr. Richard Roberts
took pictures of
fanciful magicians,

frightened but courageous soldiers,

and dedicated nurses.

Of oh-so very sad times.

Of hallelujah
happy times.

Mr. Richard Samuel Roberts
took pictures all around town.

He knew that one day
a boy or a girl like you
would look at his pictures
and see a whole world
in the eyes of a Carolina boy or girl.

AUTHOR'S NOTE

All Around Town is part fact and part imagining. For example, the older woman on page 18 really is the grandmother of astronaut Charles M. Bolden. The family portrait on page 25 is of the Roberts family. The photographs on pages 4, 5, and 14 are the photographer's children, now in their eighties and living in cities as far and wide as New York, Washington, D.C., and home in Columbia, South Carolina. On the other hand, I don't know anything about the woman who was photographed in her maid's uniform, and then with her dress-up jewelry. I don't know if that little boy had a chicken for a pet. Or if Mr. Roberts thought this would make a special picture book. What do you think?

Mr. Richard Roberts was a self-taught photographer who chronicled in pictures the rich lives of the African-American citizens of Columbia, South Carolina, as well as other towns and cities during the 1920s and 1930s. If you want to see more of his photographs and learn more about his life and work, you can read *A True Likeness: The Black South of Richard Samuel Roberts: 1920-1936.*

JeRonna — Jordan —

Fi